Superheroes Are Everywhere

BEN VINYARD

Illustrated by: Shawn Winders

Copyright © 2016 Ben Vinyard

All rights reserved.

ISBN-13: **978-1536943221**

DEDICATION

I want to dedicate this book to my brother, Brad Vinyard. You have done so much for my life. You are my best friend and I wanted to make sure everyone could read your story.

Everyone knows someone that they think may be a superhero. Well, my big brother is a super hero, and I even have proof!

Have I seen him fighting crime? No!

Have I seen him in his costume? No!

There is more to being a superhero than wearing a cape or fighting bad guys.

Being a superhero is about protecting others and always doing what is right.

In the summer time, we spent a bunch of time at our grandmother's house and we played outside a bunch.

We spent a lot of time playing in the woods, rode our bikes around the neighborhood, and played a bunch of video games.

Our favorite thing we liked to do was to build tree house forts. My brother was very good at finding the best trees.

I didn't know exactly what made a tree good for fort making, but my brother would always help to find the perfect tree so that I could have an amazing fort!

When we weren't at our grandmother's house, we were swimming in the park pool. On a hot summer day, this was the perfect way to cool down.

Since I was much smaller than my brother, bullies would try to pick on me. My brother would always be there to protect my sister and me.

Superheroes Are Everywhere

Summer time was also good for playing baseball. My brother was the best!

He could throw the hardest and hit the ball the longest. He was super-fast, as well.

After practices, he would always take me to get lunch and made sure I got enough to fill my belly.

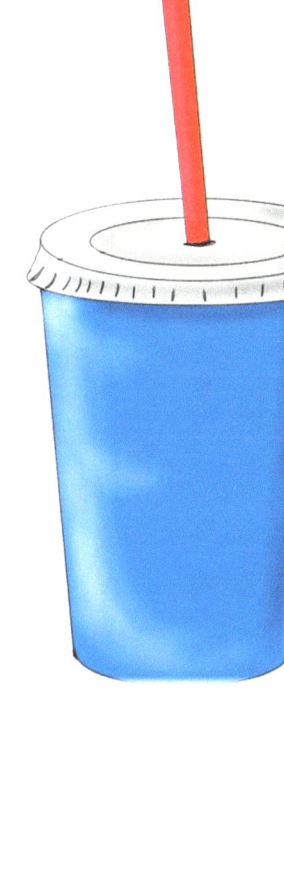

Sometimes even when you're super, you still get sick. My brother got very ill and had to take some strong medicine.

The medicine helped him to get better, but he still was not himself. The doctors told him that he needed to get a new leg.

My big brother now has a robotic leg. His new leg helps him to get from place to place, and he doesn't miss a step.

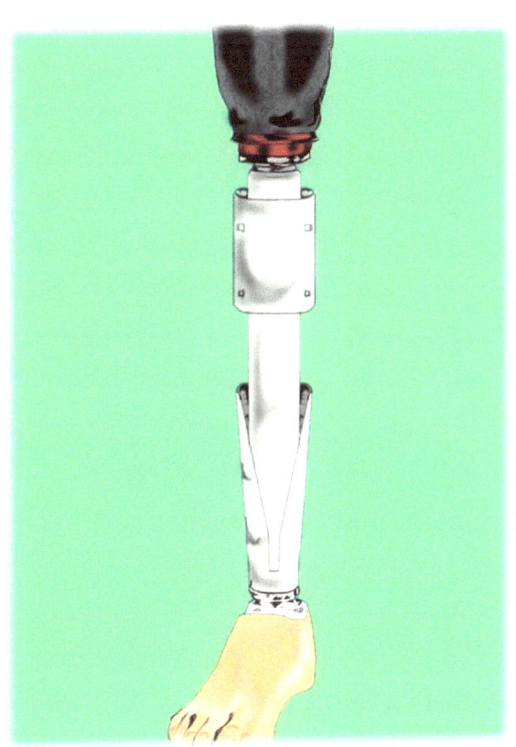

My brother has to be a superhero...he is so strong!!! He lifts heavy things all of the time!

He has big muscles and can even lift people over his head. I'm not kidding!!! I've seen him do it!

My brother is a world champion power lifter. He has set many records and has won a bunch of trophies for being so strong!

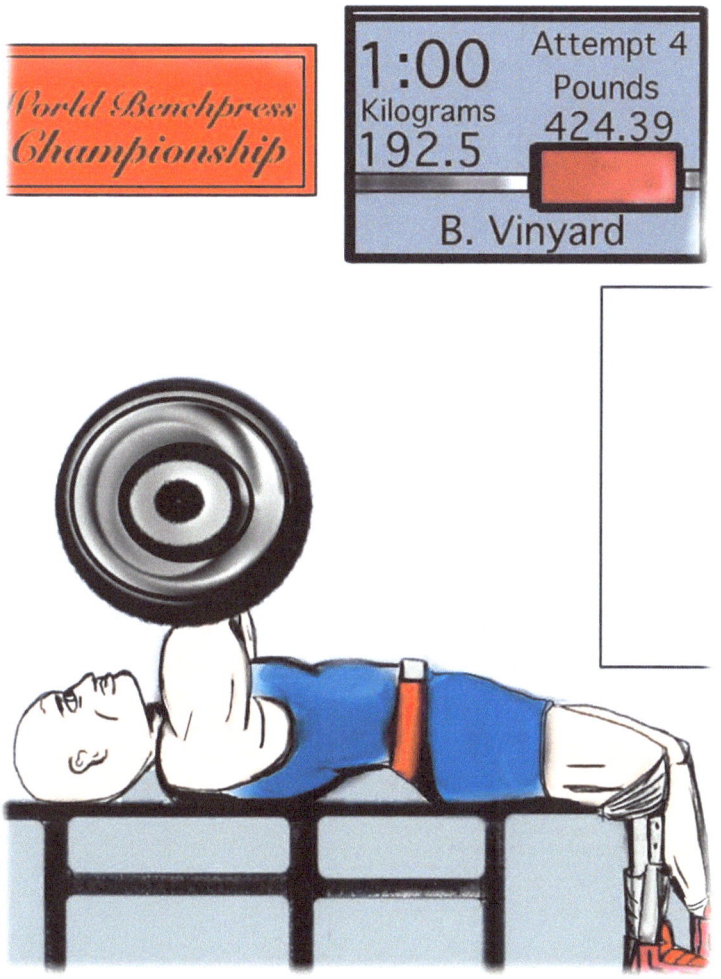

I get to watch him lift weights and have even helped him train. It's great having a big brother that is so amazing.

See? My big brother must be a superhero! He has super strength, and he's caring. Sometimes he even saves the day! I'm so glad he's my big brother!

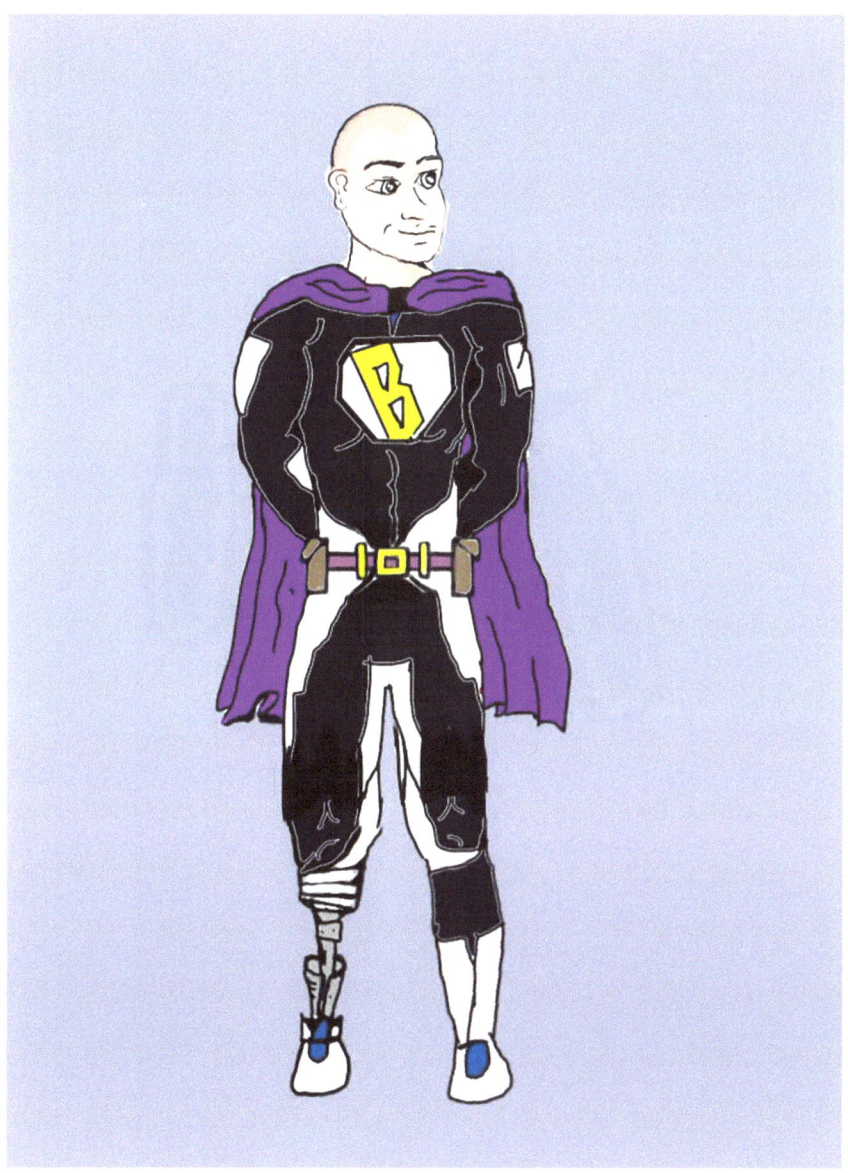

About the Author

Author Ben Vinyard was born and raised in Southern Illinois. A school teacher of nearly ten years, loves to spend time with his wife, Hilary and their daughter, Lyla. In his free time, he enjoys doing martial arts and reading. He and his family also love going to the movies and traveling. Ben's brother, Brad, was diagnosed with bone cancer in 1996 when he was a senior in high school. He has now been cancer free for twenty years. "Brad is my best friend and I wanted to show everyone how much of an inspiration he is to not only me, but to others as well."

CPSIA information can be obtained
at www.ICGtesting.com
Printed in the USA
LVHW072052061220
673491LV00001B/40